a new beginning

by

Paul Aidan Richardson

Publisher: Talulah Press

Cover Design and Artwork: Susan Mitchell

Type Set: Nick Ridley

Distribution: Zymurgy Publishing

Paul Aidan Richardson is hereby identified as author
of this work in accordance with Section 77 of the
copyright, Designs and Patents Act 1988

Printed by Angel Book Press, County Durham, UK

ISBN 0-9547410-1-3

With thanks to

Margaret

and Martin of Zymurgy Publishing

CONTENTS

Foreword   Kevin Whately 7

A New Beginning   Introduction 11

Reflections 13
Prayer 14
A New Beginning 15
Lorna 16
Birthday 17
Love is Young (A song for Margot) 18
Nostalgia Profiteers 20
Abandoned 21
What's it all For? 22
Before the Fray 23
Escape 24
A Wasted Life 25
Wrinkles 26
Tear 27
Expectancy 28
Snowdrop 29
Dependency 30
The Thin Line 31
Reflect 32
The Successful Diner 33
The Physician 34
Who will Bury Me 36

A MIGHTY SEA   Introduction 41

Secrets 43
Hope (Extract) 44
The Mistress's Charge 45
Crustaceans 46
Shipwrecked 47
On Tommy's Trawler (Extract) 48

The Survivor 49
Slick 50
Fatally Wounded 51
An Ordinary Man 52
The Drowning of Jeannie MacDonald 53
The Purifying Storm 54

Warriors of the Great Plains Introduction . . . 59

New Generation 62
And some went to the shores 63
Eagle Feather's Lament 64
Warrior Stag 66
Challenged 68
Plea to the Great Spirit 69
Understanding 70
When the Lodge Fire Dies 71
Talulah 75
Talulah - Before the Dawn 76
Talulah - The Ending 78

Foreword

It was not long after meeting Paul in the 1960's, before I realised that he was, and still is, endlessly inquisitive, has enormous enthusiasm for life and does not believe that it should be a single straight path. He goes off along the bye-ways and immerses himself in his latest interests, often for years.

Indeed the poems, as presented in this his second book, follow very much the course and influences in Paul's life.

The first section reflecting very much his early upbringing in a rural Vicarage, his father being the larger-than-life Reverend 'Jack' Richardson, whose life and career were the subject of the best selling "Jack in the Pulpit" books. Working as an 'unofficial curate' has influenced his writings, as I know that he was constantly questioning and trying hard, to give reason to the real fears and anxieties that people hold concerning their lives, the reason for their lives, and eventually the aftermath of their lives. Many of the poems are thought provoking so I am pleased that Paul has lightened this particular section with the interspersal of gentler poems, for example A SONG FOR MARGOT; WRINKLES; BIRTHDAY and TEAR.

The Sea has always been a motivating factor for Paul. 'Jack' had been a Naval Chaplain and his brother Malcolm died while serving as a Marine Engineer. Paul was himself a serving Reservist on HMS Calliope in Newcastle, he later became a dealer in Marine Paintings and Artefacts, and, for a person who is habitually sea-sick at the mere smell of the oceans, has endured some harrowing experiences while sailing in some of the most ramshackle boats afloat! Like many of the old-timer fishermen in Northumberland Paul's respect for the sea is unshakeable.

Paul has an extraordinary thirst for new experiences, and ponders constantly what he can put into life as well as what it can give him, so his quest to know and understand better the history of the Native Americans comes as no surprise, and, knowing Paul, neither is his need to rear and train American Quarter Horses. The basic belief, by these Horse Plainsmen, of a Universal Spirit can also be seen in the previous two sections, albeit in a different guise, it represents feelings that are understandable and identifiable in us all, as such, I am sure that readers will identify themselves with at least one of the poems.

Enjoy your reading.

KEVIN WHATELY

A New Beginning

Introduction

Many of us will endeavour to cling to the 'status quo', a pattern of life to which we have become accustomed. However, we have the ability to start afresh, in order to gain new life or a different dimension to our lives. It is this quality or gift to adapt and change, that has enabled us to etch out our own pathways through an often turbulent life.

Even the seasons have a time for death, winter, in readiness for the rebirth of a new world, which is heralded by springtime. It is a fundamental need of creation, the idea of building something from nothing, breathing 'afresh' from the new winds of life.

For me the simplest poem in the book, 'SNOWDROP', illustrates the fact that there will be new life created in something that is seemingly gone forever. So it is, that much of my poetry ends with the hope of life, probably the most classical work being 'WHO WILL BURY ME', which was written shortly after my father's death. This theme, however, can also be seen throughout my work, in particular 'EAGLE FEATHER'S LAMENT'; 'WHEN THE LODGE FIRE DIES' and 'SHIPWRECKED'.

The necessary thought of a new life permeates my poetry, not only after death, but during the course of one's lifetime. The best illustration being 'A NEW BEGINNING', and hopefully the reader will recognise similar sentiments in the PHYSICIAN, which again illustrates an enforced change of life, albeit for a probable short period, and THE PURIFYING STORM which is a massive plea for a dramatic change.

When we have reached the end of a journey, it should herald the start of a fresh beginning. Our enthusiasm which we held at youth, may have waned; the years may have jaded our sense of adventure. In which case we must not fear sending our imaginings ahead in preparation to a new and wonderful experience.

I will stress, as I have in the past, that my poetry tends to be instant, rather than thought-out, and once a poem has 'arrived' I rarely alter the wording or formal English. I hope this lack of technical awareness will not spoil the readers' appreciation of the poems.

She patted and smoothed
Out her pinny
picked up the needles
And began to dwell
Upon the pattern of life
She had knitted
And the stories
She could tell

. . . . .

O life, what can I give thee?
O life, what is my end?
O God shed forth thy light
So that I may find myself
And be my own friend.

A NEW BEGINNING

Glimpsing the world
From her own 'Bridge of Sighs'
Reflecting past sadness
In those quiet lonely eyes.

Looking for comfort
Crying for help
Looking for refuge
From her inner-self.

She loves and doubts
Pleads and shouts . . . .

For a new beginning
The resurrection of her soul
For that, which was broken
Her heart, to be made whole.

Let her dream
The thoughts of innocents
While trustingly asleep

Let her wake anew
In your care
To keep

BIRTHDAY

The anniversary of a year
Descends in man-made time
Forget this progression of age
And let your heart shine . . .

Let your heart shine
And your spirit free
So like this timeless earth
You'll last until eternity.

*I have realised that life's great victory is not to triumph, but
indeed to struggle to the end. By doing so we should not be
measuring our lives by the calendar years, but by the experiences
we encounter. It is for us to remember that we live in
'deeds not breaths'*

LOVE IS YOUNG
(A Song for Margot)

Love is young
And too gentle to rush
Life impersonal
For your dreams to share
So hide your thoughts
Within your dreams
And leave them awhile
To linger there

Chorus.

When you're a Lady
Ambition burns strong
When everything right
Seems to turn wrong
Look into your dreams
Set in skies of blue
See the world revolving
It's turning for you.

Chorus

When you're old
And memories are sweet
Of the love
You keep in your heart
Remember those dreams
How they came true
How they're still working
Helping you through.

Chorus: Then by releasing them
One by one
Into an unknown
And hurried world
You'll ride the future
Upon your dreams
Your banner of life
Proudly unfurled

Leaving belongings
Scattered like his ashes,
And bought by random
Profit makers, who
Catch life's dust and
Recycle the lost memories

ABANDONED

I've heard the screams of victims
Echo and re-echo around
And the deserted worked out seams
Vibrate with that mournful sound.

It is the speakings of the past
The rumblings of miners' souls
Who cried for new tomorrows
Salvation from their black holes.

No longer do those black arteries
Pulsate with the throb of Hewers at work
And with the rise of murky waters
The coal no longer crashes to earth.

It's a requiem for those who died
In those deserted worked out seams
Who like their flickering lights
Were extinguished, along with their dreams.

Will this be the end
The triumphant Amen
When boys go to War
Returning as Men
When women will weep
'Till they cry no more
Begging to ask
What's it all for?

BEFORE THE FRAY

He smiled
The whimpering smile
Of a man afraid

To sing
A simple song
To a merry tune played

With laughter,
Spontaneous laughter
As in a child's charade

But knowing
As all men know
That the Dawn will fade

The life,
Of a man living
To die alone, afraid.

Is this what I have lived for?
A place at heaven's gate
The pleasure of drinking from the cup of plenty
And food served off a golden plate.

Or is it all a wistful dream
That came upon me unexpectedly
When, on turning life's corner
I stared into the face of reality.

A WASTED LIFE

As the agony of reality
Blinkers her eyes
She sees her world crumbling
Amidst the constant lies

She won't let go
She can't let go
Of the fragments of love
Which have been her life
Cemented her Being
Made her a proud wife
"Oh what a fool I've been
To have wasted all these years
Sacrificed my heart, my laughter, my tears

Now, like sand running
Through a broken timer,
I am unable to repeat
That which I have lost
As emptiness has replaced the promise
My soul left to count the cost".

Wrinkles help frame a smile
And give sympathetic eyes
Show that you care for a world
Revolving on an Axis of Sighs.

TEAR

Take a tear as it falls from your eye
And see the rainbow formed within
Kiss it away, with a heart-felt sigh
Before the magic colours fuse and dim.

Watch it drop into a river of time
That flows into a mighty sea
And catching upon the currents of love
Starts a voyage that ne'er a man will see.

This is a story of replenishing the world
With colour, light and love
Of how your rainbow helps us all
With just a little help from above.

The hand, no longer trembling with age,
Instilled with calm expectancy
Is gently laid upon the sheets
Feeling for the final comfort
That life can afford.

SNOWDROP

O snowdrop, how did you arrive?
The Earth so barren
The bee still in the hive.

O snowdrop, where did you go?
You can't be gone forever
For you didn't say 'cheerio'

Where can I see beyond today?
In a Land where dreams
Are not blown away

I have no life
It is on his I have to cling
Just a pair of empty eyes
And a love song
I cannot sing

Oh, where can I see beyond today?
In a Land where dreams
Are not blown away

THE THIN LINE

The silhouette of a lonely man,
Hides the pleading of a circus clown
Behind the veneer of this perfect sham
He cries and laughs, smiles and frowns.

And under this frail veil of confidence
Lies the exposed, supposed man
Scratching the surface of life
While silently yelling, 'I am who I am!'

Give this man the peace you can afford
And mark his presence with a strengthening force
For without his lacquered hardened skin
He'd lie bleating 'My Kingdom for a Horse'.

Reflect...
As the pools reflect
With a rippled clarity
The moods of Heaven.

THE SUCCESSFUL DINER

I drank from my youth
To give sustenance to my age
Ate the crumbs of my happiness
That I might be fulfilled.

But my napkin was soiled
By the stains of the love
That had dropped during courses
From that Table above.

THE PHYSICIAN

He watches the crumbling edifices
Of a human mind,
A numbing brain
Grappling with the latest find

'But I have so much more to do
So much to give
I'll treat each day anew
If only I can live
Longer than what you say
Why, o why, this determinable day ?'

'I haven't got the answers
I can only at best delay
Mortality is given by right
Its not for me to take it away

I can only conjure
With the very stuff of life
To enhance the quality
And remove the bodily strife.

'Sorry' is such a pitiful
Word to say
But try to give others strength
By what you experience today

For 'whoso suffers most
Hath most to give'
Think not of death
But of the life you have to live'.

WHO WILL BURY ME

Who will bury me
Where the whisps of time
Mingle past and future
Old and new
And this cold air is warmed
As darkness recedes into golden hue.

Who will bury me
Where scattered dreams are reborn
On a wind that carries
New life
And the Oceans waft their breezes
Beyond this world of human strife.

Who will bury me
Where the shoreline passes
Through the vision
Of enlightened men
Who, seeing beyond the years
Cry, 'It will be as it was then'

Who will bury me
Where I can walk with angels
In the playful innocence
Of a mighty sea
Upon which my soul will be borne
As gentle voices call, - will call me.

Who will bury me
Where the sun will never set
And all its vibrant colours
With rainbows tied
Explode to welcome new life
In one who had already died.

A

MIGHTY SEA

Introduction

The leaded skies hung with grim intent, over the snow covered mountains which acted as dour guardians of Loch Fyne. The bleak scene set in contrast the sight of a grown cob swan, swimming slowly but surely, head held erect, along the centre of the Loch towards an angry ocean.

Murdo McDonald, my companion that afternoon, had already explained that the hard, and bitterly cold winter had driven a fox to attack and kill the female (pen) swan, after a fierce battle in which cunning had eventually triumphed over the awesome power of the mute swan. As a consequence the swan's mate had, for some days, mourned the loss of his life companion and was now ready to submit to the same fate by swimming to an unforgiving sea, when, with his wings spread in final supplication, his neck would dip graciously beneath the waves to join his lost mate.

The remembrance of this lone voyager prompted me to write about the elementary moods of the oceans and man's fascination and attempted comparability with a force that will surely always beggar any attempted understanding of its works.

JEANNIE MCDONALD, in the same manner as the swan, sought an end to her despair, after the death of her beloved mate. Whereas the mariner, in 'SHIPWRECKED', who is seemingly drifting to a death caused by natural elements, knows that he will be foundering upon a rock "on which all are saved", perhaps this writing is the result of my vicarage upbringing! By contrast, however, "THE PURIFYING STORM" is sheer self indulgence.

The old mariners are never dismayed by the moods of the oceans or confounded by its basic, and, at times, niaively intolerant nature. Nevertheless, even at the height of its terrible awesome might, we can still witness a majestic and beautiful work of creation. I would like to think that "THE MISTRESS'S CHARGE", illustrates some of the power that the great seas can unleash.

Unlock your secrets
Oh mighty waters,
And tell me what you know
Tell, before the future catches the wind
. . . . And all my dreams go.

Oceans render much, except for their love
So turn to man and God above
Touch the soul of God
By looking into the hearts of men
To have their understanding
You can die and live again

THE MISTRESS'S CHARGE

Pale mistress of the night, with reins of water in her hands
Uses her mystical powers as the sea she commands
Teasing with scorn, disdainful and yet proud
She heralds her charge under a clouded shroud

Then whipped by wind and depression the Captive reels
As in a tormented body for the shore she steals
Set on a course of anguish and pain
That only the mighty headland can contain.

All conquering, save of God's own might
The phalanx moves by day and night
With columns trailing their streamers high
Like the mist of souls rendering their final cry
Before once more retreating into the deep
Laid low to rest in an eternal sleep.

Her course run, and rage complete
She turns in defiant, obedient retreat
With boundaries defined and Land conquered once more
She bids farewell to a battered, scarred shore.

Ask the crustaceans what life
Is for

Because they helped build this
Encrusted shore

With their bodies laid
To rest

Poured their innards into the
Ocean's breast.

SHIPWRECKED

Wash my soul to distant shores
For the tempest, that has run its course,
Looted my spirit, and breached my soul
Now bellows its quietness with penetrating force

And as the veil of fog is drawn
O'er the dying, shrinking sun,
That sheds forth death's red plumage
Heralding the final day done

This spent voyager, drifts into a sinking sleep
Towards a tranquil Ocean, in a timeless grave
Life skimming before him, as he founders
Upon that Rock, on which all are saved

... The watery gleam of the boat's spotlight
Penetrates the salt air and diesel fumes
Making the oil-skins glisten
And, as the rain, driven by wind,
Slices hard into our volatile nautical Keep
To rid the scene of clinging entrails
The gutted remnants of Ocean's harvest
Trawled and hauled, reaped from the deep...

THE SURVIVOR

Time will not wait
Time will not care
Time will do its best
To end my life there

So I'll not fear the wind
And I'll not fear the waves
I'll hold on tightly
While everyone prays

For Time ends everything
Except for itself
Me - I'm a survivor
Needing only God's help.

Endeavouring to preserve the life
That breathes her goodness,
The Ocean coughs up it's spirit
With oil choking gulps,
As the clotted shadow crawls
To clad itself to the shore,
Like an abhorrent Angel of Death,
Bidding welcome with a black, suffocating claw.

FATALLY WOUNDED

Empty beaches and
Headlands with nothing to protect
Sand-dunes that stand stark
Against a world
That time wants to forget.

As the tumbling
Billowing clouds,
Their menace contrive
To roll the badness from
That hole in the sky.

Which bleeds
The tissues of existence
Flowing scarlet against the sun
As the eye of the vortex weeps
For what mankind has done.

For this is the end of an ordinary man,
No mountains did he climb
Nor miracles perform
But the world should be grateful
For the Day he was born.

THE DROWNING OF
JEANNIE MACDONALD

I thought I heard an old bell toll
Way out there in the mist
Echoing through the hanging shrouds
Vanishing in a time, that no longer exists.

And before the night stills the march
The harbinger calls once more
Pacing its vibrant message
Onward, toward a stark, petrified shore.

Spreading the reverberating ripples
O'er the still waters of the Bay
Where once widows were sought
Their menfolk swept away.

Give up your Dead, O awful Sea
And let those who mourn walk free
For the young girl who cries in vain
Lives to be reunited again.

To a Love, who was taken from her side
A Love who now calls, so that she may abide
Within thy bosom, dark and bare,
Deep she sinks to meet her lover there.

THE PURIFYING STORM

Guide my penitential soul
Over an ocean
That leads to a barren peace
Where wind and sea
Will etch out my life
And engrave my spirit
Upon that mast
Which, though heavy with strain
Carries before it a billowing life
Amidst the ravages of time

So, at the height of the tumult
When all seems lost
The sea will unlock its secrets
And I will look at the reflection
Of my own despair
In the towering wave
Which will engulf my mind
And tear at my very existence
Like a ship torn apart upon a reef
Formed by the final cries of ancient mariners

Yet I know, as the sun
Disappears into the darkness of the waves
Swallowed up by a solitary colour
Into absolute obscurity
Taking its life
And rendering it forgotten.
That a new tomorrow will arise
Buoyed by a primary force
That, although quick to temper
Is all forgiving

So the calmness of the waters
Will temper my soul
Bidding me welcome to a new World
And a golden sun
Will light up my eyes
Which will reflect the warmth
In the myriad colours of the ocean
And the very pulse of the deep
Will be my heartbeat
Its strength my inspiration

WARRIORS

OF THE GREAT PLAINS

Introduction

I stand five feet nine inches tall, talk with a thick Geordie accent, and walk with a slight limp; notwithstanding, no-one can convince me that I do not walk, talk and look like John Wayne, indeed, get me into a western saddle and I AM John Wayne!

Acquiring a saddle was easy, however, I have to admit that it looks a lot better strapped to a horse, than straddling the back of the best settee. In short, I was compelled to buy an American Quarter Horse, whose ancestors have graced the silver screen in every 'Cowboy and Indian' movie ever since Roy Rogers gunned down his first badman.

So it was to my old buddy, Jay Mele, who I turned for help and advice upon the subject of buying a suitable horse for this tough, dust-biting hombre.

Jay is a throw-back to the old West, speaking with a slow cowboy drawl, each word seemingly weighed with great wisdom and the experience of his six decades of hard cowboy upbringing. It can only be the lure of the smell of fresh coffee that will entice his tall, lean frame from the back of his horse, occasions when he is able to impart his profound insight into life's intricacies, while at the same time, rolling a fresh cigarette, a practice he can equally perform while riding the most difficult of horses at a generous lope. His Stetson is never removed, even at full gallop against the strong northerly winds his hat stays firm.

Jay now manages a ranch near Ausable Forks, a small town situated in the northern area of New York State, a two hour car journey from Montreal Airport. The winters are harsh and bitter in this region of North America, so any horse that I was to buy should be as tough as the great steeds that have created legends in the West.

Thankfully Jay had dismounted before calmly striding over to my bed and waking me at two in the morning, in order that I could witness his best mare, quite harrowingly named 'The Widow's Sister', giving birth. So, suitably dressed in just about everything that my suitcase contained, as protection against the piercing cold wind that was drifting the snow to the very height of the barn, I made my way inside, and sneaked as close as I dare to the sweating mare, in order to gain comfort from the warmth that she was radiating during this her hour of deliverance.

"Paul I want ya to meet the vet, 'Eagle Feather'." So pre-occupied with my own wellbeing, I had not noticed the tall gentleman with the long neatly brushed, grey hair, and with eyes and mouth smiling with a freshness and caring that I am sure went beyond even that expected from his profession.

"Wow!" Is all I could say, like a young child, mouth gaping and eyes enlarged to twice the size. I instantly forgot the time, cold and foal trying to extradite himself from his mother's womb.

"I've always wanted to be an Indian, or rather a Native American!" I hastily corrected.

Eagle Feather, while carefully checking the placenta, that had a few seconds earlier encapsulated the newly born, after the long and complicated birth, smiled.

"Oh, you don't have to be an Indian to feel the spirit."

That was my defining moment. I was totally entranced and, during the next two hours, while mother and baby bonded and Eagle Feather was able to satisfy himself of the foal's health, he regaled Jay and myself with the stories and history of his ancestors. How, pursued by the Cavalry, they made good their escape from their beloved Great Northern Plains to the safety of Canada, only to be thwarted by the very elements that now ravaged the outside of the barn, and were turning a varied and beautiful landscape into a hostile white cauldron in which it was impossible to imagine anyone surviving.

Hearing such stories told by Eagle Feather in such an atmosphere, place and time, could not help but leave an impression so deep-seated that, soon after my arrival back in England, the poetry reflecting the endeavours and hardships of the Native Americans flowed freely.

I have selected a few of my personal favourites for this particular section of the book, including 'EAGLE FEATHER'S LAMENT' and 'WARRIOR STAG', however in order not to make the reader too thoughtful, I have included the love poem entitled 'TALULAH' which means 'Leaping Water'.

Eagle Feather is correct when he says that you do not need to be a Native American to feel the Spirit for he truly believes it is universal and, as such, I hope that the poems will touch a cord within you, the reader.

As a footnote to this introduction I have to mention that I am the proud owner of 'Poco Eagle Feather' (Little Eagle Feather), who is now a fine young stallion, and lives a good life under the care and tutorage of my good friend Jay.

There is a new generation of old men
Carrying before them the wisdom of time.
But as the sun sets, they are quietly gone
And their voices are heard no more . . .

AND SOME WENT TO THE SHORES . . .

The salt caked furrows
Chiselled into the face,
By an awesome wind
At unrelenting pace.

That sculptures earth and soul
With identical hand
Leaving the dead and Living
To become a handful of sand.

EAGLE FEATHER'S LAMENT

I can close my eyes,
And still see the lands of my ancestors.

I can sleep,
And still hear the cry of my people.

I can close my heart,
But still feel the lament of the Buffalo.

I can wash my spirit,
Yet my eyes still look to the mountains.

For there is a place
Where the eagle soars
Upon the winds of hope.
Where I will be governed
By Nature's laws
Running free with Deer and Antelope

I open my eyes
And fill my heart
With longing.
I can sleep
With the great spirits
Without hearing my people sobbing.

So I will return
To the great Northern Plains
Where, upon a pony, my spirit will ride,
Knowing there's no longer a need
For the vanquished
to hide.

WARRIOR STAG

Fixedly staring
Brown against green
Wary to move
Until his intruder he'd seen.

Then pivoting
His two powerful hinds,
Moved gracefully for cover
Behind the tall pines.

'Great Warrior of the forest
I ask you to forgive
For my family grow hungry
We need your life to live.

The North Wind blows cold
The snows will soon be deep
I offer my tears
For today your family will weep.'

'Great Spirit of all
Let my arrow run straight
So death will be sure
And there's no time to hate.

For like this mighty warrior
Whose story will never be told,
I will die forgotten
Before I grow old.'

Know that if a man is not challenged
He becomes empty, and lives a lie.
Like a pool, which is not replenished
He will become still and die.

PLEA TO THE GREAT SPIRIT

Is this the way of my people
That I no longer see a lodge for my son,
Do the hopes of my fathers
Evaporate before my work is done.

Give me one more night to dream
That our nations are one,
That my lance, which grows heavy,
Shall be held high by the strong.

Let my arrows run true
And my shield protect.
Let my pony, which grows weary,
Harness courage with the strength he has left.

When my spirit roams the plains
May my tipi still stand,
Give my Son the wisdom to know
That defeat was never planned.

As the playful
Babbling brook
Runs gently into a fast
Flowing river
That replenishes the waters
Of a mighty sea.

So the thoughts
Of our children
Will be the inspiration
to their fathers
Whose knowledge will enlighten
Warriors like me.

WHEN THE LODGE FIRE DIES

When I am old
I will walk in the paths of the young
When my legs no longer support my body
My mind will soar with the eagle
When the great Chief has no more mountains to climb
He will discover a new summit

For as the warrior looks for life in death
And the child looks for the prancing deer
On a deserted plain,
I will look for a Beginning
When I come to the End
Lay down my lance
And call my enemy, my friend

"TALULAH"

TALULAH

When the North wind blows,
She is my shelter.
When the winter snow falls,
She is my warmth.
For her smile is the spring,
Her laughter the summer.
She is my season,
And my reason.
She is the dawn
And the going down of the sun.
She is the one I love
Beyond the days
When my life is done…

BEFORE THE DAWN

The young braves are restless
Their ponies painted for war
They cry a song of freedom
Believing its worth dying for . . .
And I will stand with my people
To fight for a new Dawn
So the ways of my father
Are enjoyed by the new born.

Hear my words
That they may be with you
Until the end of your time,
When our souls will meet
Our love entwine.

My Lodge has been blessed
By your presence

My mind made fruitful
By your Belief

My strength nourished
By your Goodness

My Heart warmed
By your Love

You are my Being
My comfort
My stay
I will always be there –
Beside you
At the Dawn of every Day

TALULAH - THE ENDING

I bend the knee
And fall to the earth
My eyes no longer seeing
But showing the growing hurt.
My pony lies still
No longer able to run
Among Warriors like me
for whom songs are seldom sung.
My Spirit will catch the wind
And there, like an Eagle soar
Toward a new tomorrow
Where pain is felt no more.

I only have dreams
To offer my son
My words for you to hold,
Treasure them forever
For I will not be there
To watch you grow old.
So look on me now
With a forgiving eye
For I know, as Death
Honours the Warrior,
The Spirit of my People
Will never die.